SPECIAL EDUCATION

SPECIAL EDUCATION poems

Caroline M. Mar

TEXAS REVIEW PRESS • HUNTSVILLE, TEXAS

2019 X. J. Kennedy Poetry Prize Winner
Marilyn Nelson, Judge

Established in 1998, The X. J. Kennedy Prize publishes one full-length collection of poetry each year.

PREVIOUS WINNERS

Garret Keizer, *The World Pushes Back*
Jay Udall, *Because a Fire in Our Heads*
Jeff Hardin, *No Other Kind of World*
Gwen Hart, *The Empress of Kisses*
Corinna McClanahan Schroede, *Inked*
Ashley Mace Havird, *The Garden of the Fugitives*
Jeff Worley, *A Little Luck*
James McKean, *We Are the Bus*
George Drew, *The View from Jackass Hill*
Joshua Coben, *Maker of Shadows*
Ashley Renee, *Basic Heart*
William Baer, *"Bocage" and Other Sonnets*
Becky Gould Gibson, *Aphrodite's Daughter*
Deborah Bogen, *Landscape with Silos*
Lee Rudolph, *A Woman and a Man, Ice-Fishing*
Eric Nelson, *Terrestrials*
Jan Lee Ande, *Reliquary*
Jorn Ake, *Asleep in the Lightning Fields*
Barbara Lau, *The Long Surprise*
Philip Heldrich, *Good Friday*
Gray Jacobik, *The Surface of Last Scattering*

for my students, with gratitude

Printed in the United States of America

Published by Texas Review Press
Huntsville, Texas 77341

Library of Congress Cataloging-in-Publication Data

Names: Mar, Caroline M., author.
Title: Special education : poems / by Caroline M. Mar.
Description: Huntsville : Texas Review Press, [2020]
Identifiers: LCCN 2020004445 (print) | LCCN 2020004446 (ebook) | ISBN 9781680032345 (paperback) | ISBN 9781680032352 (ebook)
Subjects: LCSH: Women teachers—California—San Francisco—Poetry. | Multicultural education—California—San Francisco—Poetry. | Asian American lesbians—Ethnic identity—Poetry. | Women with disabilities—Poetry. | Cultural pluralism—Poetry.
Classification: LCC PS3613.A68 S64 2020 (print) | LCC PS3613.A68 (ebook) | DDC 811/.6—dc23
LC record available at https://lccn.loc.gov/2020004445
LC ebook record available at https://lccn.loc.gov/2020004446

Cover photo courtesy Flickr

Contents

When You Someday Read This—

I took your story, held it to the light
like a glass I was checking for flecks
before putting it, tidy, on the shelf.
Forgive me, if you can—

Naming you what your mother did not
name you. Hiding you in the name
of protection, making your stories
one story. Holding your story

against my mouth for so long,
smudging its glass with my thumbs.
Breaking its glass in my mouth, your mouth,
our mouths as we chewed

through our stories.
I have taken your mouth.
I listened, not carefully enough, spelled it
exactly wrong. Forgive me everything
you thought you could trust me with.

Forgive me: what I've forgotten,
what I wasn't ready to say, what
I never knew. Inside your opening mouth
is a story, and I'm waiting—

for you to speak it, glass everywhere,
broken and ringing, that old
American sound.

I. LANGUAGE LESSONS

Chinese Girl

Bing bing. In the mouths of my Black students
my ethnicity is the sound of an elevator rising
past the floors of some anonymous downtown building
they will never set foot in. Our security guard,

also Black, uses *Chinaman* instead,
which I'm busily un-teaching
alongside the elevator's ring.
My aunt was a teacher too, called her boys

hak guai, as my grandmother called my mother
bok guai. Devils of two colors, but devils
nonetheless. And I was simply *quai*.
No Chinese family praises

too much its favored child, old fear
of covetous demons. My students now,
likewise naughty, troublesome, trembling
not with fear but laughter

at racial terms thrown about our room.
To them I am something else entirely—
a teacher by any other name
is still fucking white-acting.

My kids want to know what kinds of women
I have loved. If I've ever dated
a Black woman. They don't know the word *butch,*
but they know *stud*.

I suppose I could tell them about the woman
I wanted to go home with, spring break
in Jamaica, the fear afterward.
The young men hosting me imagining

I had talked to another boy
(apparently, they didn't know the words
butch *or* stud). And considering the way,
the night before, the brother of my assigned fling

flashed me the gun he packed
into his waistband, nothing like
the strapped-on packages I'd wanted to touch
on butches and bois back at school

who thought I was too straight-looking, I knew
if they found out the truth we might get hurt, really hurt
by these boys who called me *Chinese Girl*.
But on second thought

flings and bars probably aren't what I should disclose
to my kids. Happy marriage. Safely gay.
When the driver's buddy in our Beijing "black car"
started asking me, *tong zhi, tong zhi?* I didn't know

where we were, or what time it was, so I gave my girlfriend
a look that said *silent*, and I said, *ting bu dong,*
ting bu dong, no, I do not understand you. Waiting
for the safe escape into the hotel's glass doors

and swift, silent elevator up to a quiet room
that held one double bed. Not telling them

about spending years as the sweet roommate
to my future wife, chatting politely about the Virgin Mary

or the patience of being a special educator
with my future father-in-law, who tells me,
I've been watching this minister on TV, last name Kim,
I think he is Asian, and *Do you know him?*

The way that closet collapsed, and suddenly
we were both on an express elevator to hell,
e-mails full of hate and anger, and me
no longer anything even human to him.

Everyone wondering how he could have missed it,
his butch daughter who for years
never brought anyone but a woman home,
his deluded hope that I might wield

a feminizing influence, before I became nothing
but race, sex, sin.
It's a pretty good day, if the kids are just asking
what kinds of women I've loved.

They just want to know who it is
I really am. What shape my name should take
in their mouths. When I finally get home,
I will look my wife in her eyes unlike mine

and will wonder but will not ask,
When you look at me, what do you see?

Ghost Language

My grandmother, the white one, my mother's mother, she has
Alzheimer's.
It isn't an easy thing for Grammie, or my mother, or me. My
grandfather,
the Chinese one, my father's father, it was the same: he lost his English,
then his mind;
the ghosts all came to pace his hallways.

Things I know about ghosts: the haunting, of course.
We bring Grammie mini-candy bars, the tiny shiny squares of sweet
she loves,
and honestly it might not be so terrible, a quick and painful heart attack
since she's forgotten
she wanted to end it before things got this bad.

That sometimes, ghosts have voices. *I was . . . I was a smart woman*—
a writer, as deliberate in her choice of words as in her choice of
pearls.
Her language never failed her. My students speak a language I don't
always understand. It rings
of false bravado, a high-striker hammer dropping to prove some
mewling manhood.

That ghosts spoke to you more clearly than I could, at the end.
I teach the code's switch, the value of speaking both vernacular
and academic, the only way they'll make it past entry level at Foot
Locker. But also,
the way those ghosts were welcome, and weren't you happy to see
them,

so happy to have back all the people you'd loved, together, like a
reunion.

I am supposed to value their home language, the way my father,
ghetto-C-Town born, still says, *It's mines*. She does. Does. Not "do."
Goddamnit, just speak right.

And you, somewhere in between.
But worse than awful conjugation is hate of self, that word I cannot say—
Ghost voices flutter. They whisper, flash, flicker the lights, fuck with the volume
of the radio. When you have dementia, it's like your brain goes backward.

You remember who's important, but not why. Some days, my mother
is Grammie's lovely niece, and I might just be the light brown help.
My friend Mika used to see ghosts as a child, until she learned to make offerings
many times a day. Or maybe she just grew up.

N-----. They tell me, *It's okay! We are allowed to use it*. The semantic difference
between "er" and "ah" unleashed from all our history.
And also, that they float, according to Western tradition. I think in China,
ghosts walk and talk and hide themselves in the bodies we are used to.

I read an article about the n-word in Grammie's *New Yorker*, back when I was a little
younger than my students are now. I'm no great student
of folklore but know ghosts can't step over, that every door should have a block.

The author had a point, but I tell them their argument fails in the face of my words,

Chinaman and *chink*, say nothing of the dear-loved *queer* and *dyke*.
White people ghosts would breeze right through those walls you built.
I forbid the n-word's flutter in my room.
This works, for short periods of time.

In my West African dance classes, we talked a lot about the ancestors gathered
behind each dancer. I don't know what else Black ghosts do. Haunt
the white imagination? Hang around my classroom, nudging
these boys forward, eyes rolling gently at every young mistake?

I take Grammie and her "friend" Fred out to coffee. The osteoporosis makes her small
as a child, feet dangling, her latte's foam as patient as I am with her repetitions.
Fred talks because he can remember. *You know, there's a good Chinese restaurant near here.*
Grammie's eyes narrow in concentration; I can almost see her reaching

for the memory. Chinese food. Chinese people. This brown girl
in front of me. Family. That's what I'll do—come back and sigh, again, again,
speaking while no one hears, a gossamer of disappointment, a sheen
of sheer hard work: my best language for love.

Wasn't I? she asks, looking first to me and then to Fred, forgetting
the daughter who became the mother that birthed me,

that daughter's wedding, her whole life,
    Was I *married to a Chinaman?*

When it happens, it's like I leave my body.
    Who am I to you?
When you hear it, old ghost, so many times a day, it starts to seem
    normal, really,
    until finally, it just happens—

it just slides into your own mouth, as if you might speak it, as if it
    didn't break your heart
    while you clench your jaw.

The Bear

When she screamed, I thought it was a child.
Later, she would refer to this sound as a "schoolgirl" sound,
which is—I'll admit—what it sounded like. But I dislike the
connotation
of weakness and young womanhood, to scream like that. It probably
isn't
the sound I would make, being wiser about these things and not new
to the idea like she was. I would like to think I'd have shouted,
stood tall, clapping my hands—
thok, thok, thok

But this is just what I imagine. And anyway, even if I would have been
butchier in my choice of sound, is that some sort of judgment

on what sounds emerge from what bodies
who sings and who sighs
who whispers and who lisps

It was what she had wanted,
in a way, kept wishing it, and then it happened, and I should have
gone with her, but she said no, and how was I supposed to know
that she wanted me to insist—

When it happened, I thought it was a child. Then, I thought
she must be witnessing it, and how exciting to get what she wanted.
To see it like that. And I wasn't that worried about the child.
I wasn't even worried about her.

It was in the quiet, after, when I opened the screen and looked out
at darkness I could not see into—
that was when the fear came.

Fenway, Boston Red Sox versus Cleveland Indians: Kosuke Fukudome

at bat. Watch the little brown boys
admire their daddy's freckled girlfriend
as she fakes a Japanese accent. Watch
daddy, laughing—*tough name*
to pronounce. Set aside, for now,

frustration with his team's name,
harder to bear than his, certainly—or your own
memories of your beloved Grandpa Joe
telling WWII stories about *Japs*, after he helped you
fraction out your identity, pie-chart
of segregation. Wonder

what has happened
to their Asian mother.
Watch them, eyes full—
of what? It can't be love.

Passing

after A. Van Jordan

[adj.] Going past; (of a period of time) Going by; Carried out quickly and lightly; Meeting or surpassing the requirements of a course of examination. [n.] The passage of something, esp. time; The action of throwing, kicking, or hitting a ball or puck to another team member during a sports match; Use euphemistically to refer to a person's death; The end of something. Not included: (of a person of color) Deliberately or passively being (mis)perceived as white.

As in, the grades you gave all students
during the Vietnam years, to keep them
from the draft. My first experience, *Wait,*
you're not white? Your blood in my veins.
Your glance over Grammie's face, loving,
the passage of a marriage spent in lockstep,
intellectual partners, a bond of more
than mere affection.

[n.] A gentle feeling of fondness or liking; Physical expressions of these feelings; A condition of disease; A mental state, an emotion.

As in, the affection you wouldn't show each other
in public, but I knew was there. She gave back
another man's ring to be with you. You wouldn't
show my mother, either—but to me, all.
The plaque that spread silently through your veins
squeezed in on you through angioplasties,
the quadruple bypass, finally the stroke
that killed you—would this be an affection of the heart,
then, the veins, or the blood, or the brain?

[n.] An organ of soft nervous tissue contained in the skull of vertebrates, functioning as the coordinating center of sensation and intellectual and nervous activity; The substance of such an organ, typically that of an animal, used as food; Intellectual capacity; A clever person who supplies the ideas and plans for a group of people; A person's mind; An exceptionally intelligent person. [v.] Hit (someone) hard in the head with an object.

As in, my brain, the most important part of my body
to you. Your crowning achievement, the flash cards,
the tape recordings, the IQ test at age three, all to prove
what you could make of me. Long car rides
exercising math facts, history. Showing me my first
human brain (was I six? eight?) at the college,
floating in formaldehyde, squiggly and strange,
beautiful to you. What brought you and Grammie
together, your smarts, your matching
PhDs. The steeliness of your intellect, logical
and hard. Hard to imagine you, moments
as a boy, gleefully cruel, the pain inflicted by a hard hit
at the expense of your younger brother; I only remember
you yelling once or twice. At the end,
unplugging you, the only soul you believed in
already dead. Your body finally yielding.

[adj.] (of a substance or object) Giving way under pressure; Not hard or rigid; (of a person) Complying with the requests or desires of others; Giving a product or generating a financial return of a specified amount.

As in, what your heart never seemed to do
for sadness. The table always set for formal dinner,
my father calling you *lace curtain*. Only once,
being interviewed for ninth-grade history homework,

your voice opening to a crack
of briefest sorrow—the men in your memory
calling for their mothers as the ship went down.
My mother unyielding as you, facing off, fifteen,
belt in your hand, a man I cannot imagine,
even if it was only a threat. The gene I mutated,
your training creating only a rebellious streak
in an otherwise oversensitive child. What you left me,
multiplying, first college, then grad school, the apartment
I lived in, the house I own free and clear—
more privilege than your depression childhood
ever imagined. The way you weren't,
when I picture you at Vietnam protests.
The yielding of the crowds
when you passed through.

Your Language, Your Face

after Jose Antonio Vargas

Life, it has been—what?—to you. You face me, intent, eyes giving
away almost everything, that whole windows cliché, but truly, looking
past me like
America—your eyes seem at once sad, smart, brave. Or, if I spoke (pick
one: Farsi, Swahili,
Tagalog), they seem—no, that's not my language. And anyway, can
eyes look anything but
after something else? I could make you
caliph, or king, or someone less regaled, although peasants are rarely
entered for sitting portraits. Much less wearing bright blue stripes, my
favorite color, running
to your neck, shadowed and unshadowed, both sides, like passion
and pain, or other things that are not opposites, but still have
difference between them. Like the half of your face that is marked,
twice, and the half that has not
one blemish, tear or tear. I wonder if what made your brow hard was
school
like it is for so many of us, or if childhood rolled right past you
and it was the grown part that was hard, leaving behind the simple
spelling of your name, the easy way to carve your sign into stone or
sand, what no one
can pronounce. Is there a word for what you left behind?

Tongue

Things I remember: Mamah's voice,
loud and clear, the language I spoke,
then forgot, then spoke again, and have now

almost forgotten. The way I would transliterate
the words for my mother, one-hundred-character
test prep. She would read my letter-words, all sound

with no meaning, and I would write them down.
I would check my own work. I always
check my work, and you should too.

It is the best test-taking strategy. This will be
on the test. Everything is on the test.
Yeyeh was asked, at Angel Island,

how many steps to his neighbor's house. How many
chickens in the yard. At least, I think he was.
I have taught history, I know these were

the standard questions. What answer is correct?
I have no chickens in my yard. There are fourteen
stairs to my front door. No, thirteen. No, there were

fewer stairs if you went through the back door—
it was easier on Mamah's bad knee. My father's stories
about that staircase, childhood tumbles,

frightened me. It all bleeds
into one story. I don't remember how it ends.
I don't know yet. Make sure you follow along.

Death of the Immigrant Language

First, I went to get some dim sum.
I was so hungry. Good-byes and tears and watching
the mortuary van pull away
will do that to a person. And when I walked in to order, *mm-goi,*
yut goh ha gow, facing the usual lady with her streaky grays
across the stainless-steel counter, that's when I realized
no one will say my name again.

I will not use these words again, except to ohdah food.
The counters are kept clean of grease and rust.
I wish my mouth could do the same.

I will not hear you say my name. I will not hear,
except in passing, a few words here
and there—the bus, the market,
the shapes and sounds that could fit
on one postcard: all I knew how to say
to you, anymore, and even that makes no damn sense:
good-bye-see-you-again

Body

I never ride the bus without a book, some purpose
to my waiting between here and there, a way
to fill the time with things more important
than the journey. And yet I am distracted, always,

by the cacophony the bus presents, the conversations
I am allowed to watch and hear: the queer kids
talking about threesomes, the punky andro-
butchy girl sitting on the lap of the femme-y

hipster boy, talking as if the rest of us aren't there, loud,
about her sex with women not him, which girl is hot,
who gets to watch, if he'll be allowed to touch
or not, interrupting my reading of whatever book

or magazine I had that day, forgotten as I wonder
if all that's coming from her loud gravelly voice
isn't a performance as much as her double-sided lip-
piercings, her blue and black bihawk, the chunky

way everything hangs on her solid frame. Listening
to them, I don't feel young anymore. I know
it's frivolous to say I'm old. I am nowhere near
the grinding down of my body past any point

recognizable, the body finished. When Joe died,
I was wrecked. The way his body kept
moving, the forced gasp of a bellows inside his chest,
his breath the last thing to let go of him, the body

trained for its work even after the vent shut off.
The nurse said it could take hours. We left.

What else could we do? Listen to that noise
until it extinguished? So we left him there,

and I was grandfatherless. He and Grammie
should have gone together, holding hands,
their breaths slowing easy. He waited too long.
After the cremation I cleaned their house,

the hoarded morphine, the right-to-die
literature packing their file cabinets. He had missed
the window of opportunity. The time you get
to decide. Watching Grammie go alone: years,

it took her, asking where Joe was, then asking
what his name had been, then just waiting in pain
for everyone to leave her alone. When we said good-bye,
all that was left was her rattling breath, gurgling

from her wrinkled throat like a coffeemaker. I couldn't
shake the simile in my head, so I said it, and we started
laughing, snot and tears and laughter at the sound
of mornings, the suck and release of a snore

with water running through it. I wanted to read to her
poems of dying, peace, love—but I couldn't
speak, so I read to myself. Weren't they really for me
anyway? Everyone wants some solace, someplace.

I say everyone as if having a body is always
so easy. As if the body can't be transformed.
I spend hours reveling in the reshaping
of other bodies: *RuPaul's Drag Race*, how much I love

the sparkle, the shine, to judge each queen her queenliness.
How well they pass. How much interest for passing.
How at another poetry reading, *important* and *significant,*
we were crowded into the back room of the bar, sparkling

lights on the stage, genderqueer and transfolks reading
about how they are more than their bodies. Be honest—
I was thinking about their bodies, what choices were made,
how much T, transition, and time went into crafting

this body or that. And how white. And how strongly
I reacted—that shade of privilege
doesn't suit you, hunty—
to every transman's word about a woman's body,

when one poet read about rescuing Gretel and I thought,
Motherfucker, don't you know that little girl was the one
who pushed the witch into the fire?
Who wants all that masculinity, I wonder? My wife

will strap on a dick beneath boxers, wear a blazer,
bring flowers when she picks me up for a date, lift me
into bed when I call her handsome, handsome. I never said
I was a logical person. Why else would I love poetry?

Why else define my body's slide against the body
of another woman, joy loud as the queer kids on the bus?
Pushing their bodies brash into my shoulder
as they exit, while I go back to my magazine, wondering

why the "inspiring" photographs of artsy writer's magazines
are always black and white. Grayscale makes up the bodies

of brown women on display—strange, exotic, unique
as whatever they are selling. Two young girls balance

one atop the other, head to head, flat sequins shining
against their leotards. Children practicing their act,
the little one probably not even dizzy anymore.
The base girl, older, has eyes that focus somewhere off,

ignoring the camera that captures their moment.
Behind them, the edge of a circus tent, ground,
as they hold their arms balanced like mirrors,
round heads connected by a cushion of hair.

Pages later, another photograph: a woman,
her hair covered entirely by iguanas, a crown
of the living lizards, many gazes asking, asking—
I can't know what that spiky crowd is thinking.

Maybe it is market day. Maybe it is a celebration.
Maybe she knows the turistas love a good show. She looks
directly at the camera; it is the iguanas who look away
and out. I am tired of reading.

I put down the magazine, look out
the window. A mother climbs onto the bus, settles down
with her newborn. She chats with the man
across the aisle. The baby is three weeks, the baby

is a girl baby, the baby's head will not stay wrapped
in the swaddle tight to her mother. *Oh yeah, she nosey,*
she so nosey, always want to see what's goin' on. She wants to be
another body in the world, in the world, another body.

II. PRIMER

How I Got Them

1—My third week of teaching, seventh grade, drilling for earthquakes. *You will all be so quiet, and you will duck and cover quickly, and we will walk in line silently—the* most *quiet class—and I will be so, so proud of you.*

But, when the drill sounds: every
child screaming from below
the desks, laughing faces howling
up at me. The clipboard crashed
down, splintering. The awed
silence. The awful
words: *Ashamed. Ashamed.*

2—Year one, in the hallway, and the art teacher beelines for me. *I cannot have this class. You have to help me. I have all* your *kids in there and they are too much.* As if I birthed them.

A week later, in view of thirty kids
and another teacher, she slams
the door, walks out—
I have too many
SpEd kids in here!

Nothing happens to her.

And to them?

3—Not the fights. Not my coffee cup, arcing through the air, brown splatter across the floor as the kids hoot with delight in the chase. Not the desks squealing out of the way as bodies crash into them. Not the thump of feet, knees, elbows, skulls against linoleum. Not the phone call, voice even and calm: *L3. We have an L3 in Room 311.*

4—*I really think he might be a sociopath,*

whispered between us teachers. Later, across
the conference table, parents denied
everything, said he was wonderful
at home, it was just school.
Thought maybe we were making it up,
or just didn't like him.
Your son said he was going to punch me.
He called me disgusting and said
I was going to hell. He sat cornered,
unsmiling and unrepentant. Of course
I didn't like him.

5—*Damn, look! Miss has hella gray hairs. Miss, Miss—are those because of us?*

Because about 66% of students receiving Special Education services are boys, and in our school's self-contained SpEd classrooms that number increases to about 99%

Because I am the only girl,
I will not talk to you. Because I am

the only girl, I will hate
most of my classmates with a passion
fiercer than the hissing notes *stupid,*
dumb ho, hey hey hey they whisper
past the ears I try to hide inside my hoodie.

Because I am the only
girl, I will put my head down on this cool smooth desk
if I want to, refuse
to write, to read aloud, to work. I will draw
massive looming sad faces over and over
on any paper you give me, because

I am the only girl. I will be lonely
all the time. I will be quiet. I will
wait patiently for you to help them—
squealing greedy boys—until now, when my need
pitches up and out of my furious throat
and I am screaming down the endless beige
of this hallway, banging on a blue locker because
you never listen to me.

Secondary Trauma

> *Secondary*: inferior in rank or status; not of major importance; depending on or incidental to what is original or primary; of or relating to secondary education

> *Trauma*: injury: any physical damage to the body caused by violence or accident or fracture, etc.; an emotional wound or shock often having long-lasting effects

I found these definitions online, Princeton's
dictionary. Which is where the new teacher went
to school, actually. Before teaching here.

He came into her classroom, asked
Aren't you afraid? Which fear—
his hands around her neck, or worse?

I'm going to punch you in the uterus.

These are things we cannot say to a student: *No.*
I'm going to punch you, first in the face and then
in your pubescent testicles, for being such

a fucking woman-hater I want to cry
and scream and slit your savage throat.
You can't say those sorts of things to kids, at work,

when you are a teacher. She wouldn't
anyway, of course, she's very sweet
and from Texas. She knows

how to follow the steps. She will file the police report.
The principal will suspend him. I will hold the meetings
to determine whether his crazy is excusable

or not because of all the terrible shit
that's happened to him. But what can she do
when she lies down in her bed alone

and his voice—*that voice*
that I fucking hate—that I hear in my own
dreams—it echoes back.

When are we not afraid?

Special Education

1. AUDITORY PROCESSING DEFICIT

I say now is not the time for this conversation.
You hear shut the fuck up, dumbass.
I say open your books to page 253.
          You hear open.
          You hear books.
          You hear page. But never
                    at the same time. You say,
what? I say the same thing
over again, *rephrased or restated for clarification.*
          You say, what?
I say look at the picture,
or the written instructions, follow along
in the notes.
                    You say okay, I got it
                    already.
I say your disability affects how you think
about the things you hear. I say pictures and writing
and reading help you learn.   I say you need to double-check
the things you think you hear
other people saying.   I say look
at me.
          No, at me.
                              You say I don't need
these special classes.
                              You say fuck you,
I'm not fucking retarded.

2. EMOTIONAL DISTURBANCE

The last time I saw him was the day
he ran up and down the hall, kids egging

him on as he dodged police we'd called because
he'd eaten out of the trash can again,
my trash can—
                    a sandwich dipped in paint,
yogurt cup full of old water, pencil
shavings. When I asked him why he liked it:
because there is already somebody's
saliva on it. When I asked him why
he did it: *the voices*. When I assigned
homework, "imagine your life in ten years,"
he wrote, *I hope I am not homeless.*

3. CONDUCT DISORDER

I dread your arrival, even
as I am tasked with your safety.
How can I do my job
like this? Even your freckles frown
in oppositional defiance.
I want to resist you, hell-bent
on hatred, your bitter-metal voice,

I call hurt babies herpes.

I throw my head back
and laugh, then the other boys laugh,
you are laughing, getting
what you wanted and maybe
what you didn't—it's not
that I hate you, though sometimes—

Who could need more than this?

You are mine,
my ugly little love.

4. VISUAL PROCESSING DEFICIT

This is how it is: I'm watching your mouth move, the gloss
around your orderly teeth, square
and symmetrical, lined up like little blocks, the patterning
to their click and close,

while you tell me about this or that
child in crisis, and I hear you
with only one ear, while in the room
over your shoulder, behind my eyes,

I am visualizing the certain cascade
of Tetris tiles, sliding into the spaces made for them—
the holes left open—
falling into perfect place.

Idiom

Those who can, do, and those who can't . . . You know
the rest. Everyone knows this saying, or is supposed
to remember this or that slice of idiom, to share
a *cultural schema,* or even care

about these little phrases. Not my students,
if I had to guess, the way my co-teacher
and I guessed so well at a game of Taboo
that we slaughtered, as a team of two,

a team of ten of them, mostly immigrants,
ELLs, for whom a shared schema was bent
useless, since it did not include
Monica Lewinsky or *soap opera* or even *blue*

jeans without a pause, thinking hard
about every answer for every card.
So much choice: what to say that wasn't forbidden,
what might come through in a fast association—

English-first and English-best,
English-only on the English test—
I counted out a slowdown of my fast brain
as co-teacher and I tried, tried to slow the train,

to level the playing field. *Well, hmm, I don't know,*
there are so many ways I could go
here, he stalled for time, and in the gaps I stalled my mind
with fear and failure: theirs and mine—

a tangled net of all the ways I've let them down,
the ways the world will let them drown—
No: the ways the world will try
to drown them. It doesn't matter if I cry.

Tears won't be the thing to unmake
a world that wants from them, from me,
what we can't give: conformity,
a world I half-times want to break,
and yet, the world I replicate.

The Fix-up Strategies

a collage

Readers sometimes get stuck
when they read, not understanding:
a word—

you say you a gangsta but that don't impress me none—
or losing the train of thought: the difference between
a good and a poor reader—

you say you a gangsta, ain't seen a thing you done.
Many students do not realize they are not
racial and ethnic disparities. Understanding

in graduation rates. Is that the good reader?
Disappear.   I know you've been hurt
by someone else.

Realizes that comprehension has
                                        broken
                                                down.

When students of color master reading?
What they read?
So?

Teachers must help them when they veer
off course—
They realize it

by the end of third grade.
And are not living in poverty.
I do it all on myself; I ain't getting help,

becoming so engaged in the text that
roughly 85% of children diagnosed
with learning difficulties have a primary problem:

Fuck you. I'm not fucking retarded.
With reading and related language skills,
most children with reading disabilities

can become proficient readers. They schools
can't teach us shit. My people need freedom.
We tryin' to get all we can get,

and immediately know how to correct it.
All my high school teachers can suck my dick
and can learn strategies for success

in school, tellin' me white man lies and knows
what strategy to use to fix it.
Straight bullshit, I can tell by the way

you carry yourself.

Ask Questions

What state do we live in? What country?
What is four times four?
What are your favorite books?
How do we each learn best?
Who are your best friends? Who makes you
feel less alone in the world?
What are your favorite foods? How is food important
to family cultures? What happened to your father,
your mother, to you? What were the causes
of the French Revolution? What does "revolution" mean?
Why are you angry? Can you tell me
an example of an adjective, like "angry"?
When will you stop fighting me?
Who hurt you? Who still does?
Where does it hurt? Where?
Why wouldn't you be angry? How
can I possibly make this better? What do you need
to be able to trust me? What do you need to survive?
Are you hungry? What state
do we live in?

Reread the Text

NO. She's so stupid.

I don't know why I got sent out of class. I got
sent out because The Beast hates me!

She started yelling at me and said I said
something but I didn't say nothing, she's crazy,
she says I said but I didn't say and I don't know
what she's talking about.

I didn't do nothing wrong! But she didn't
believe me anyways!

Next time maybe The Beast should listen!
Next time maybe I will call her a beezy
to her crazy Beast face.

I only feel mad. I'm not
learning anything. What about
me?

Miss got mad at me.

She said I was talking. She said
I called her a bitch.

I did not call her a bitch.
When she started yelling I didn't say
anything.

She told me to leave, so I left.

Next time I will apologize. I know
she was hurt and that's why
she yelled. Next time
I will put my electronics away
so nothing can be mistaken
for my voice. Next
time I will be silent so she cannot
blame me.

Yes. No.

Read the Author's Note

Sometimes I think I could use a meeting, you know,
someone says *let go and let God,* but

I don't really believe there's any god
in a classroom. On good days, a shimmer—
hope? triumph? No miracles. Good days,

I go home tired like any other. Bad days,
the work presses in on the spot where my heart

is supposed to live. Bad days, I numb up on TV
and Candy Crush, the way my kids numb up on weed,

the way other teachers knock back wine, or whiskey.
Sometimes I think: I could use a meeting. I know

I go home tired like any other. These days,
no matter how tired, how numb, I cannot quit
my racing mind. I cannot see the point

of letting go, what it feels like to let—anyone.
There is no one else. I do not accept. I cannot change.

Look at Pictures, Illustrations, Charts, and Graphs

1

Projected on the wall, a map,
each school a dot. Colored
in codes of the standardized test:
there's *basic*, taxi-yellowed;

proficient, *advanced*, the colors
of wealth. But not my school
nor each nearby. In our neighbor-
hoods, fire burns, blood pools:

below basic, *far below basic*.

2

At year's start, the principal talks
of who we serve, and who
we fail. As always, numbers: *far*
below basic, *below*,

below the tip of the iceberg,
metaphorical, blue,
in her PowerPoint. This is not,
unlike half our staff, new.

But then she tapes up photographs
on a blank, white board. Shows:
This boy, jail. This, expelled. This boy
just gone, to where, don't know.

So by the end, it's nearly half
our Black male students. They
gaze at us from shadowed portraits,
flattened to grainy gray.

3

The young white man presenting has
a passion I could squeeze
into a drinking glass. He says,
For Black students, this is

the worst place in the state to get
an education. Now
I need that drink, its sunshine wedge,
to squeeze into the low

and fizzing whisper of a G
& T, to touch, to eye
nothing but glass between my hands,
here, where color decides.

4

Some smile, but most practice the shape
of hardened mouths and eyes.
These boys are gone. We let them down.
It's quick: I start to cry

and by the end, I'm shaking, sobs
while paisley tissue packs
pass round to my sweating hands. How
deep, I wonder (don't ask),

will this water get? Far below
the iceberg's metaphor,
far past the clink of ice, I see
films of the ocean floor

I showed my kids, who tried to love
nothing, but loved the glow
of creatures alive at ocean's depths.
The water's color, though

really none, can reflect blue, brown,
or green. If you go deep,
its hue looks black. In science, they
learn black's no color. Seep

of color's absence. These boys, lost,
are failed and failing. What
shade is this disaster, then, what
color our failure's cost?

Ask for Help

after Gwendolyn Brooks

The place is a classroom. Boys with eyes shining like
pools calling themselves goons, n----s,
playas. There are only
seven since this is Special Education. One teacher
at the front of the room. Reading
the words off her clipboard. Afternoon light
golden, the teacher bearing her lesson like a
shovel. Or hammer. Or saw. Some type of tool necessary.

• • •

We don't need this goal shit. For
real, bruh, why you keep asking me the same shit? I'm
cool. Just postin'.
We ain't trippin' off no career. I'ma have *stacks on deck, goons on deck.*
Left? Whatchu mean what's left after that? Money. Man, fuck this
school. Fuck this bullshit lesson too.
We don't need none of this.

• • •

Lurk isn't the word I'd use, but Miss said it. This feeling lurks, keeps
me up
late. I'm afraid, but I'm not saying shit to nobody.
We know what's coming: bars or bullets. Don't ask me 'bout life after
twenty-five.
Strike that match, pass that blunt, because when the police tell you lie
down, damn
straight. You do what those mothafuckas say.
We can't be thinking about the future. If I do, I have to think about
getting out—

• • •

Singing rap lyrics isn't academic language, boys. No, this isn't about judging
sin. This is about deciding who you want to be in your lives.
We have a chance to work hard in here, learn our history, maybe change it.
Thin lines hold you between success and failure. Goals can be your en-
gine. How else can you know where you are going?
We need to talk about it—who do you want to be next year? In five? In twenty?

• • •

Jazz music during quiet work, Herbie Hancock just noise to them. Biding time until
June. Who wants it more: them, or me?
We keep circling. Who'll back down?
Die-cast in their molds of masculinity, I wait to find the way in, hoping for a new tool,
soon. I'm afraid I see no future in their eyes. Even when I look deeply.

Stop Reading

If you don't know it, it does no good to just
make the sounds as you go. If you don't know it,
you may never know it. We are not saying
you are stupid. We are simply saying
you learn differently. It will always be hard for you
to keep up in school. You may never
master your math facts. But you can get a calculator.
You may never write well, but you can get
a computer. You may never
pass the high school exit exam, but you can get
a waiver, and then you can graduate anyway. There are other things
besides college. You can learn a trade, make good money.
We imagine you like to work with your hands. You may never
learn to read.

III. EXAMINATION

"The Key to Saving American Education"

Newsweek, March 2010

Fire the lazy, the sloppy, the weak. Fire
the meek, those without classroom
management, without class, without
room for lesson planning
in their busy social lives. The angry,
the time-biding almost-retirees, the bitter.
Fire the (we know they will be) quitter.
Those who smoke weed, those who bring
coffee with more than a bit of Irish
in the morning. Fire the dealers,
definitely. Fire the ignorant, the complacent,
the young, and the old. Fire the bold.
Do not forget those who want too much
reform, and those who don't believe
in change. Remember to fire
those without a range of skills. Those
who threaten, who hit, who aim
to maim the children's self-esteem.
The flirtatious, the sexual, the perverse.
Those who don't know their inverse property
from their acute-angled pain. Those who
blame. The overtired, of course,
and the rushed. The complainer,
the whiner, the exhausted. The ones
who think they are always right.
Definitely anyone nonwhite.
Go first for the unionists,
but not all at once, or someone
might notice. Fire the criers, the needy,
any who fuss. Fire the ones the kids
really trust. Fire those who hate
the testing. And those who teach
to the test. When you're done, fire the rest.

Post-racial Ghazal

The snow could be a metaphor for whiteness.
My marriage could be a metaphor for whiteness.

Here is what won't kill me: my non-blackness.
My what are you, anyway. My almost-whiteness.

When we carried the baby out into it the first time, so eager,
he cried as it hit his face—such coldness, such whiteness.

The latest viral video: cop tipping the wheelchair off
the curb, crosswalk looming, screen gone to whiteness.

I've often wondered what it would be like to die
in the snow, covered in a whiteness that feels like blues—

You undo it. You undo it, I'm sobbing, you fix it,
so I am not so alone in the face of your whiteness.

Another Black body drops in the blue-black night.
At work: we have to start talking about Whiteness.

Sometimes, on the mountain, I fall. Everyone far ahead
of me, my slow turns through the wide, sparkling whiteness.

I don't want it to be personal. I don't want it
to be my story, our story, inescapable whiteness.

I know his daughter, another body angry as I am
careening down a hallway, *get your white-ass hands off me.*

She worries, through tears, that our relationship
will not survive it. Her whiteness.

When I panic, I feel like I'll stop breathing. Consider
not breathing, succumbing to the bright light's whiteness.

There is no snow left in our yard. We mourn
the losses of a changing climate. We miss its whiteness.

We never call each other's names. I love you,
baby, as we lie down, finally, in the darkness.

Blazer

Rana Plaza factory collapse, April 24, 2013

It was the place that made me. It was the place
where I came stitched and sewn, seam
to perfect seam. I am precisely

what I was made to be. I hang straight, the sheen
of my tuxedo-edged lapel shining
in the slightest dusty light of your closed closet.

I remember the hands that flew me quick and sure
up one side, around the cuff, then off
to another pair of hands, swift, moth-like

as the flutter of my striped lining was laid
within me. Blue and white stripes run
my well-lined sleeves, under buttons punched on

so fast I couldn't feel the puncture. They must
have felt such pain. Can you imagine it?
You know the whirring of the spools. The sound

of both our childhoods. Every gorgeous
cast-off blouse, irregular, snuck home
in your Yeyeh's delicate hands.

You have his fingers. It was
the place that made me. Now I am here,
in your home-place, and they who threaded

my every inch are ground to rocky dust.
The heavy hum and rumble stopped.
Let me out of this dark place. Put me on,

my mourning color. What,
did you think you would not feel it?

Ritual

In the woods, the air is cool, damp.
I love the way the earth smells, decay
of old redwoods, soft hush
of some prehistoric morning. I remember

waking as a kid at camp after outside
overnights, those most exciting nights, how
my nose would itch with the dust
of the dirt beneath my sleeping bag.

I can't ever breathe right. But here,
in the woods, cold even on a hot day
(and yes, I usually hate being cold)
the damp on my skin and in my lungs

is what it is supposed to be. My feet pad over
uneven dirt, the twining roots. Looking
up and down at the same time, unsteady
gait and sweeping gaze. We will do this

again, and again. Each time you will sigh
and smile at me. I will smile a little-kid smile
that must make my eyes look to you
something like the joyous color this rusty

pine-needled earth looks to me. Every time,
your same sweet exhale. You take my arm. Say,
This is how much I love you.
Is this love, to do the things we do not love

for the things we do?
Ferns unfurl like draperies. Trees
so tall I could lie down between their roots,
stare straight up in wonder

like the city kid I am.
I cannot name a single thing
beyond its common name.
Redwood. Fern. Leaf. Love.

The Bees

which are colony-collapsing, which are my love's greatest fear, which
are the bringers
of honey. The bees, which are, which are, which are—

for now. I could romanticize the bees. I could make them icons
of feminism and collectivization, or socialism,

but they are workers in service of a queen. Or, fuck that,
some patriarchal scientist named her *Queen*. Maybe she's just

the bee who has the job of baby-making. What is so queenly
about that? My love wants no babies. My love

is afraid, above all, of a persistent buzz in her ear,
says she could live without honey for all eternity

if the bees end up dying. *Don't make us pay*
for your trauma, I say. But I wasn't there, can't imagine

the cloud as it buzzed, the onslaught and thrum
alive in the swarm as it swam through the air

tangled in their girl-hair, glittering stinging
screaming running, the whole earth alive with the bringing

of pollen, of honey, of pain.

When Someone Screams the N-Word from the Next Campsite

FUCK YOU explodes
from my fast mouth.

A *sorry* sounds, genuine
as a blade against a wound;
the fire burns. We watch it

consume the wood. Someone
else's laughter—

We try to recover the evening.
Savoring smell of woods and smoke,
look up, look at those stars,

the black lace of the trees against
the bluer black of the sky, white

lights strung in unrecognizable
patterns we cannot ever name.
Stars and pines unshaken,

as always. *This is why I hate*
leaving the city, our drinks

clinking and sharp, the smoke
burning our eyes. The press
of someone else's good time

on my slowing breath,
I have no faith, I think—

look at those glittering stars, the quiet trees—
in what?
The trees stand; the breeze shifts.

Uniform

after hearing Ta-Nehisi Coates speak

Long gone in rot, decay
of the warm Virginia ground, swelter
of summer. Riddled

with wormholes, I can see it
in my mind's eye, hanging
in my grandfather's closet, though

I know Great-great-great-great-grandfather
was buried in it.
Memory inhabits

our heritage, the way
you spoke of imagined whiteness
binding together

slave owners, slave-
owner aspirants, as Great-
great-great-great grandfather

must have been, to be buried
in beloved
Confederate gray. I imagine

the cap, crossed rifles
resting above a placid, generic,
dead white man's face.

How fast
decay happens
in humidity's hug, that embrace

I love to walk into
when I leave my own cold
hometown. My body

feels built for the heat, like
my mother's freckled body, our old
Virginia line. I don't even remember

his first name. I imagine
the bodies that fell around him
and his drummer-boy son,

then his grandson, great-
grandson, fighters
in every major war

of this democracy
you spoke about.
I have not gone to war.

My mother's daughter,
our bodies never acclimated
to the damp cold

of my fog-locked city,
the Pacific's wind-drawn
blanket. I am a daughter

of a nation whose heritage,
you said again, is *plunder*.
I remember the brown body

of my father, the way
he angled toward me
after we sold the house,

when he told me
I should keep the money
for myself. Just in case.

How the fog
plunders the sky for space.
Because marriages, sometimes,

do not work out, because
my wife didn't come
from money, and who's to say

that what is mine
is truly hers. What vow,
what promises matter,

when you're looking at that
kind of bounty, like the wet earth
blooming sunflowers, where once

there were graves. To hold
a piece of dirt, or a dollar,
or a human being, say:

*this here, it belongs
to me.* I imagine the bodies
of my Virginia relatives

at the last family reunion.
I was curious, but too fearful
to attend. What if

I was the only brown body.
What if I was not, what if
there was tension between the Black

and the white McDonoughs,
or what if the white ones tried
(they always try)

to enlist me.
What if we met under a tree,
a spot of shade

in the unbroken heat,
a resting place,
that tree where once—

I do not want to imagine.
You said
being moral was easy, said

we have to consider
what is just.
I imagine the uniform

again, hanging cold
in a cedar-scented closet.
I imagine the smell

and the heat on my face,
distorted from flame, burning
that house to the ground—

my fingers still stroking
the textured wool, the fragile
fraying, the moth holes.

After the Pulse Orlando Shooting, My Wife Asks if We Can Eat at Chick-fil-A

We don't know yet each name for each body,
but know precisely two: one shooter, one friend-
of-friends, an old tie from your old life
and my old life, before it was our one life—
Look, look at our lives. Who would not cry
at the messes we make? Which *we* are we, right now;
which *we* do I feel most part of? We love to hate
somebody. And you, love, you love Chick-fil-A,
the warmth of every employee inside, and the warmth
of a waffle fry against your hungry tongue. No matter
if hate harbors deep inside, or high above in the command chain,
you feel the love all the same when you walk in
to that holy franchise of Jesus and fried chicken.
But me, I love the love we made
while a man strapped two guns to his body. The taste
of crispy duck, bite of bitter grapefruit, fragrance
of celebration. The clinking of our glasses:
Happy anniversary, baby. Not knowing, not needing
to know yet that *it* was happening, that by the time
it was starting, we were nestled in, repeating our mantras:
lucky, lucky. There is so much I cannot fathom.
No, I cannot imagine what it would be, to raise the gun,
gaze down the barrel, aim to kill everyone in sight.
So when you ask me, love, if perhaps today is one of those
when I can overlook the burn and raze, the rumble
in my belly, let love for you win out—
Aren't we hungry, always? Our tongues inside
each other's citrus depths, our own sweet joy a fleeting glaze
over the ash that coats my ravenous throat.

San Francisco: Boomtown

My inheritance has come in, so we have
started shopping for a house, a house
with an eat-in kitchen, three bedrooms—

one for us, one for guests, the foster kid, one
for my floor-to-ceiling books and the garish art
that overwhelms my wife so I'll have to contain it

in *a room of [my] own*, a little red-walled and radiant
office. What I want is an island of us, walk-in closets
optional, a yard for the soon-to-be dog. A rental unit

to cover the property taxes wouldn't hurt, and not
some tumbledown old man of a house
surrounded by hipsters, nor a boxy sugar cube

between Google bussers, but neither a quaint cottage
in an "up-and-coming" neighborhood where my students
overrun our stoop mornings. I want someplace flatter,

for easy walking, not like the hillcrest we live on now,
the sweeping daily vista I greet to head home, the view
across the tall skyline to the actual sky above the bay,

the beginning of the old bridge span, soon to be rebuilt,
replaced, our hilltop where the tourists always slow. Their pauses
making us wait, eager to get inside, slide the car into

our spot in the garage, run up the stairs and tumble
into the bed of the one room I wouldn't change,
letting loose the noise we are certain echoes

off the entranceway walls just out our window, letting
all the neighbors hear. And wouldn't they appreciate
our move to somewhere with more space, far away,

quiet sunny mornings for us to revel in our aloneness,
together, in the house of our desire?

Views

Our rooftop views are just landscape
and photo opportunity to them—
glittering Bay Bridge at night,
gray-white sheen of Coit and Transamerica

by day, the shimmer off the water behind cascades
of matching blonde hair on the heads
of our three tourist friends, snapping
with phone cameras a constant stream of pics

to update quickly to Facebook.
They love the white sailboats drifting
and lazy on the gorgeous bay,
my hometown built up

to layers of Victorian stateliness
and urban glamour, new glass
skyscraper condos gleaming
their bluegreen silhouettes. I love

to hate these new buildings, out-of-
proportion to this water-hemmed city
of small-scale density. From this
rickety roof deck, I can track

the steeple of St. Peter & Paul's, there,
two blocks up that hill, one over, and I see
the bed where first Yeyeh died,
then Mamah, years later, just last year,

just now I miss her, and everyone
else this city holds. What is it

to be from a place? Why nostalgia
for a place that is still my place?

Nostalgia seems indulgent,
even in this glittering light.
The visitors are smiling, laughing,
deleting what is unflattering

from the photo stream. Just before
they came, I had to take time to replace
old pictures on our walls. One is here
because she's been left again, by the woman

we were all sure was *the one* this time
around. No trace of her, the one who was not
the one, in the myriad of smiling faces
that hang near the bed I share with Sandy.

These are Sandy's friends, really,
not mine, and they are here not to relive
old heartbreaks, looking to get away
to the end of the earth, make new memories

against the Pacific's crush. *Here, here, get one
with the waves.* I comply, remember
leafing through those old photos. I found more
of myself even younger, dressed up,

with friends I don't see anymore.
The waves roll at Ocean Beach, the wind
whips blonde hair across every frame,
impossible to get a good shot.

People change, I tell myself.
People want new things, should be allowed
to start fresh. On our rides through town
Sandy drives; I am our guide:

historical descriptions, landmarks,
intricacies of who lived here first,
who displaced, aftereffects
of the Quake, the War,

Internment, or the Great Migration.
This is the part I love, telling
and retelling what makes this place.
The visitors notice most

the number of luxury cars.
I'm looking up to take in the sheer walls
of shiny new blue glass, the crush of sky
reflected in near-sky, but they

are busy counting BMWs.
If there were an earthquake,
the ground downtown would be buried
in four feet of broken glass.

Who knows where I heard this. I revel
in it, the long moment
after the sucking in of breath,
what I know is fear.

Maybe I am meaner than I'd like
to admit, a little bitter at the way

my city is changing. *My city,* I call it,
as if it knows who I am in the churn

of its reinvention. Sandy tells them
the buildings are designed for earthquake safety.
Tanks of water at the tops, water I'll imagine
as Caribbean blue like their glass

externalities, sulfurous, rocking
when the quake comes, shifting
like the city. I used to teach a unit
on earthquake safety in Geography classes.

I recall the brochures with maps of the city
I taught my boys to read: here, sand and gravel;
here, mud; here, bedrock. What if this whole city
shakes down from its own weight?

The bedrock is what stays.
The sand and gravel is what ripples
like another wave back toward its ocean.
There's more than one wave

coming over this city. How to tell it?
The words rush angry out of my mouth
as I name seismic shifts—
Bayview, Mission, hipsters, Tenderloin

Tech 2.0, that waving word: gentrification. I know
no one wants a lecture on race
in this white city. The visitors are teachers too.
This is the place they come to release

that pressure valve I can't seem to find.
To see this expanse of cold ocean.
Eat local, shop Chinatown, count
luxury cars. In the end, it's me who is exhausted.

When the quake comes, may it shatter down
like blue glitter confetti falling
from the Sunday night stage
at Trannyshack. Let that glass cascade,

rain down with my imagined water,
pierce the skylight with its shards.
Let it shake me wholly, to my very core,
or not at all.

Notes

"Passing"—This poem owes a debt to A. Van Jordan's incredible work with the dictionary as form in his book, *M-A-C-N-O-L-I-A*.

"Your Language, Your Face"—This poem was written in response to a photo clipping of Jose Antonio Vargas from the *New York Times*. The photo was taken by Ryan Pfluger. The first word of each line is text from Vargas's article; each word ran alongside/framed the photo. Thanks to Marwa Helal for the image, and for introducing me to Vargas's work.

The Fix-up Strategies—This series draws its title from a collection of strategies designed to help struggling readers that were popular among education reformers and literacy experts when I entered teaching in the mid-2000s. The collage poem that begins the sequence draws its source text from the West Virginia Department of Education's website about the fix-up strategies, Kat Dahlia's "Gangsta," a 2012 article titled "Misunderstood Minds" on *PBS Parents*, the Annie E. Casey foundation website headlines, Drake and Rihanna's "Take Care," and dead prez's "They Schools." The following six poems are each named for one of the strategies.

"*Read the Author's Note*"—This poem is a gigan, a form invented by Ruth Ellen Kocher.

"*Ask for Help*"—This poem is an acrostic. The first word of each line comprises Gwendolyn Brooks's poem "We Real Cool."

"The Key to Saving American Education"—The title of this poem was the title to the cover article for *Newsweek* in March 2010. Written repeatedly behind the title on a blackboard were the words "Fire all the bad teachers."

"Blazer"—On April 24, 2013, five garment factories housed in the Rana Plaza factory complex in Dhaka, Bangladesh, collapsed, and 1,134 workers were killed and over 2,000 more were injured.

Acknowledgments

I am grateful to the editors of the following journals for first publishing these poems, sometimes in earlier versions: *As/Us* ("Blazer"); *Cimarron Review* ("Auditory Processing Deficit" and "Because about 66% of students receiving Special Education services are boys, and in our school's self-contained SpEd classrooms that number increases to about 99%"); *Connotation Press* ("Fenway, Boston Red Sox versus Cleveland Indians: Kosuke Fukudome," "Ghost Language," "Passing," and "Tongue"); *Four Way Review* ("Post-racial Ghazal" and "The Bear"); *Lambda Literary's Poetry Spotlight* ("When You Someday Read This—"); *New England Review* ("After the Pulse Orlando Shooting, My Wife Asks if We Can Eat at Chick-fil-A"); *Nimrod International Journal* ("Body" and "Death of the Immigrant Language"); *RiverLit* ("Emotional Disturbance" and "How I Got Them)"; *Shadowgraph* ("Views"); *Storyscape* ("Chinese Girl" and "Uniform"); *The Collagist* ("Ritual"); *The Volta* ("The Bees"); and *Tinderbox* ("*Ask Questions*").

This book would not have happened without the fierce community that was ISA, a public school in SFUSD that no longer exists. Thank you to my students and colleagues there, who learned and struggled together for a place we loved so hard, even as it asked too much of us. Special shout-outs to my work husbands, Chris Cary and Keith Norman (RIP), for making me laugh in the face of chaos. My Mean Girls, Sarah Reynolds Cianciolo and Stephanie Khaziran—there's no one I'd rather sit with. Darlene Martin, Briana Visser, Kim Walker, Sean Gass, Dana Altshuler, Betha MacClain, Bill Sanderson, Rebecca Blackall, and every educator who mentored me or let me mentor them and modeled new ways to show up for our kids—my gratitude is endless. Thank you, too, to my new workplace and colleagues at Gateway for healthier and happier ways to still do this vital work. Always, always, gratitude to my students, then and now.

This book also wouldn't have happened if I hadn't had ways to get *away* from teaching. Gratitude to the Vermont Studio Center for the residency where I was able to finish my work on these poems, and to the Ragdale Foundation for the residency where I was able to find them a home.

Immense gratitude to Marilyn Nelson for seeing and believing in my work, and to everyone at Texas Review Press for making this a real object that you can hold in your hands. And thank you, reader, for holding it.

Appreciation and love to my communities of artists and writers. Rabble Collective—Francine Conley, Adrienne G. Perry, and Somayeh Shams—yes! Thank you to Ellen Bryant Voigt and Deb Allbery and the MFA Program for Writers at Warren Wilson College, especially those who taught and supported me both there and beyond—Martha Rhodes, Alan Shapiro, Daisy Fried, Maurice Manning, Rick Barot, Deb Allbery, and Gaby Calvocoressi. Thank you especially to Eleanor Wilner for being at least partly to blame for any of this magical writing life happening to me. Gratitude to the Fine Arts Work Center's summer workshops for opening the door, and to the VONA Voices Workshops, especially Elmaz Abinader's Political Content 2012 cohort, for being some of the first believers in these poems. Special appreciation to Susan Ito, the first writer role model in my life, both for being a mixed-race woman writer in the world and for inviting me to read at my first-ever poetry reading when I was still a kid. Clare Ramsaran, Adrienne Oliver, Zahra Noorbakhsh, Marwa Helal; Rachel Brownson, Nathan McClain, Tommye Blount, Lindsay Ahl, Kimberly Kruge, Kimberly Jean Smith, Jennifer Buchi; Matt Olzmann, Vievee Francis, and Greg Pardlo for the Waffle House Knowledge Sessions; Hieu Minh Nguyen, Antonius Bui, Martina Potratz, Nat Schmookler, Clare Needham, Min Shu Cheng, Autumn Meghan Brown, Maxim Loskutoff, Brittney West, Dawn Haines; and Shizen supper clubbers Susan Steinberg and Polwin Morton. My Ragdale Coven—Marcia Bradley, Adrienne Dawes, Dianna Frid, Berry Grass, Rage Hezekiah, Stephanie Kutner, Shereen Marisol Meraji, Deke Weaver, Nick White, A. M. Whitehead, L. Lamar

Wilson—thank you; your quite literal magic made this happen.

Thank you as well to my friends and family for always holding me down and celebrating me, even if sometimes you weren't totally sure what I was doing. My parents, Susan McDonough and Warren Mar; my chosen kid, Tioundra Body—from a student to our forever family, I love you; closest-thing-to-a-sister Nicole Rosendale; and my fronds forever—Krissa Lagos (who lives in both worlds), Melissa Millan, Emma Olson, and honorary frond Steven Noble. And finally, to my favorite person, wife, partner, hugger, and #2 fan, Sandy Metivier, without whom I would live in probably a lot more filth and definitely way less joy—thank you, I love you.